GET WELL SOON

Tonsillitis

Anita Ganeri and
Beatriz Castro

Enslow
PUBLISHING

Published in 2025 by Enslow Publishing, LLC
2544 Clinton Street
Buffalo, NY 14224

First published in Great Britain in 2023 by Hodder & Stoughton

Series editor: Julia Bird
Illustrator: Beatriz Castro
Design: Collaborate

Manufactured in the United States of America

CPSIA compliance information: Batch #CSENS25: For further information contact Enslow Publishing LLC, New York, New York at 1-800-398-2504.

Please visit our website, www.enslowpublishing.com. For a free color catalog of all our high-quality books, call toll free 1-800-398-2504 or fax 1-877-980-4454.

Cataloging-in-Publication Data

Names: Ganeri, Anita, 1961-. | Castro, Beatriz.
Title: Tonsillitis / by Anita Ganeri and Beatriz Castro.
Description: Buffalo, NY : Enslow Publishing, 2025. | Series: Get well soon
Identifiers: ISBN 9781978538689 (pbk.) | ISBN 9781978538696 (library bound) | ISBN 9781978538702 (ebook)
Subjects: LCSH: Throat--Diseases--Juvenile literature. | Tonsillitis--Juvenile literature.
Classification: LCC RC182.S3 G24 2025 | DDC 616.3'1--dc23

Find us on

GET WELL SOON

Tonsillitis

Hi there! My name is Maya, and this book is all about the time I got tonsillitis. I felt really ill. My throat was so sore that it hurt to speak or swallow. I couldn't eat anything except soup for a few days!

This book has lots of information and advice about tonsillitis to help you, and your parents or caregivers. On the following pages, you will find out:

What are your tonsils and what do they do?

What is tonsillitis?

How do you get it?

What can help you feel better?

Tonsillitis is when the tonsils at the back of your throat get infected. It's quite common for children to get tonsillitis, but adults can get it too. You can get tonsillitis at any time of the year.

It's the day of the class play, and Maya and her friends are very excited. They have been rehearsing the play for weeks. Finally, this afternoon, they get to perform it in front of their parents and the whole school!

First, though, Maya and her friends have the morning's classes to get through. In English, they write a poem. In math, they practice their times tables. But everyone is struggling to concentrate.

After what seems like forever, the bell rings for lunch. It's pizza today – Maya's favorite.

In the cafeteria, Maya gets her lunch and sits down with her friends. She nibbles a slice of pizza, but her throat hurts when she swallows, and she feels a bit sick. She sips some water but it doesn't help much.

After lunch, Maya and her friends head back to their classroom to get ready for the play.

They put on their costumes. Sophia and Jan have a pretend sword fight.

It's nearly time for the play to start. Maya is feeling quite sick now. She has a headache and her throat really hurts.

In the school hall, the lights go down. The music starts up. The audience goes quiet. The class takes to the stage. The play is an action-packed pirate adventure. There's a pirate ship, and buried treasure. There's even a parrot!

Maya plays Scurvy Sally, the ship's mate. She was really happy to get the part. But she's feeling even worse now.

At the end of the play, all of the pirates appear on stage to sing a final swashbuckling song. Maya has to sing quietly because it hurts her throat.

The audience cheers and claps loudly. Maya and her friends take a big bow. Everybody agrees that the play has been a great success!

Back home, Dad gives Maya a warm drink and some liquid acetaminophen to soothe her throat and stop it hurting. Then Maya goes straight to bed.

Maya's throat is still really sore the next morning so her dad books her a doctor's appointment.

The doctor asks Maya how she is feeling. He feels Maya's neck, and looks down her throat. He uses a special flat wooden stick to help hold Maya's tongue down so he can see better.

The doctor tells Maya and her dad that Maya has tonsillitis. He shows them a helpful picture.

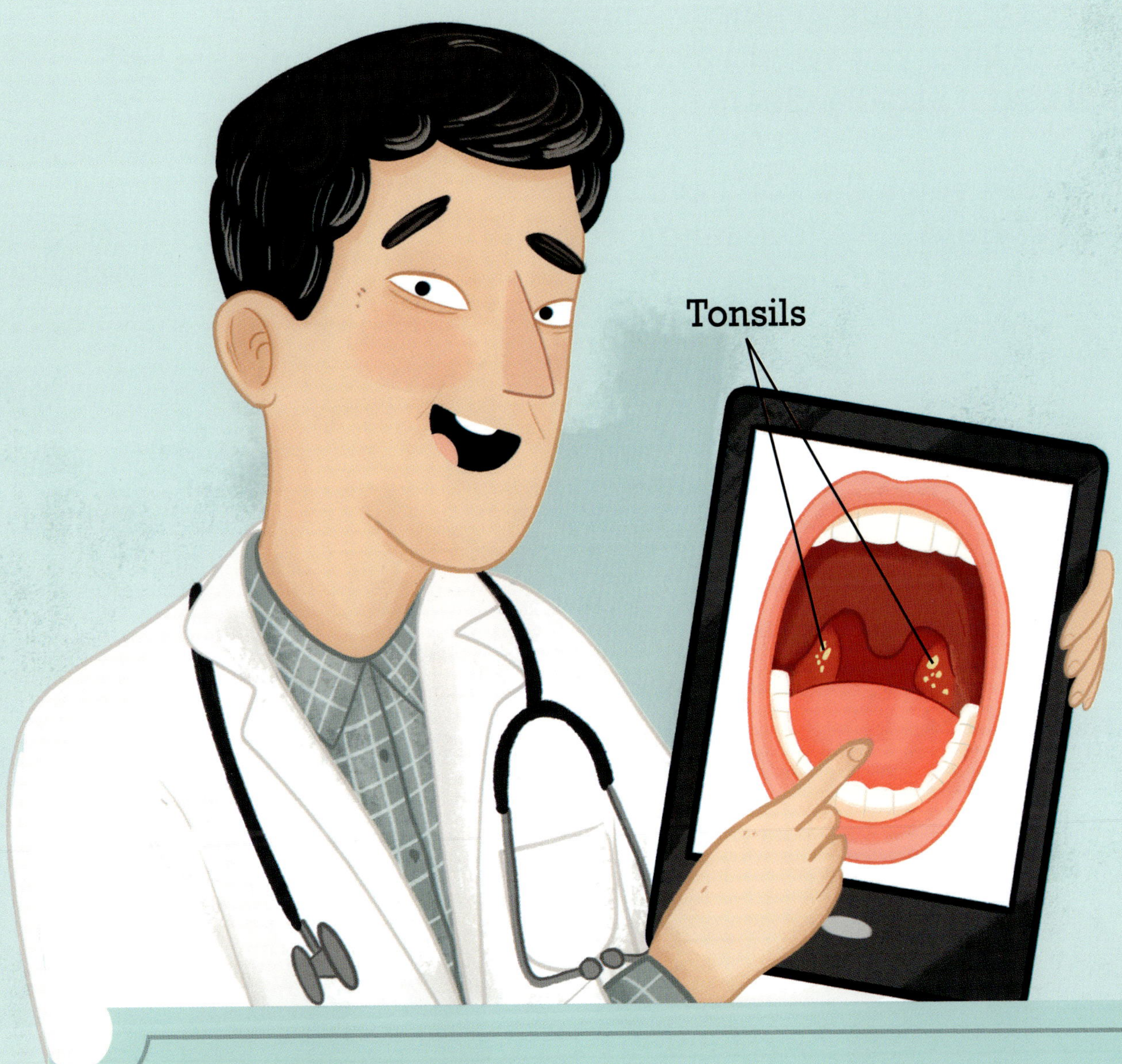

TOP TONSIL FACTS

* Your tonsils are in the back of your throat, one on the left and one on the right.
* Their job is to fight off germs that come in through your mouth or nose and could make you ill.
* Sometimes your tonsils can get infected and become red, swollen, and sore.
* When this happens, it is called tonsillitis.

SYMPTOMS

Tonsillitis is a common illness, especially when you're a child, and after you've had a cold or the flu. It can be quite painful, but it usually clears up by itself in a few days.

So, how can you tell if you have tonsillitis? Here are a few things to look out for – these are called symptoms.

If you have tonsillitis, you're very likely to have a sore throat. But having a sore throat doesn't always mean you have tonsillitis. You can get a sore throat when you have a cold or the flu.

VIRUS OR BACTERIA?

One kind of tonsillitis is caused by germs called viruses. Another kind is caused by germs called bacteria. A doctor may be able to tell which kind of tonsillitis you have by looking in your throat. If you have little white spots on your tonsils, you are more likely to have tonsillitis caused by bacteria. The white stuff is pus. Your body sometimes produces pus when it's fighting off germs. Pus contains dead cells and bacteria.

If you have tonsillitis caused by bacteria, the doctor may give you antibiotics to take. Antibiotics are a kind of medicine that kill bacteria. If you have tonsillitis caused by a virus, antibiotics won't help. They don't work on this kind of tonsillitis because they don't kill viruses.

When the doctor examines Maya, he feels for painful lumps in her neck and under her chin. These lumps are swollen glands. They swell up to help your tonsils fight off germs.

The doctor tells Maya that her tonsillitis is probably caused by a virus. It should clear up by itself in a few days.

Make sure you get plenty of rest. That means no school for a few days.

Drink lots of water to keep you from getting dehydrated.

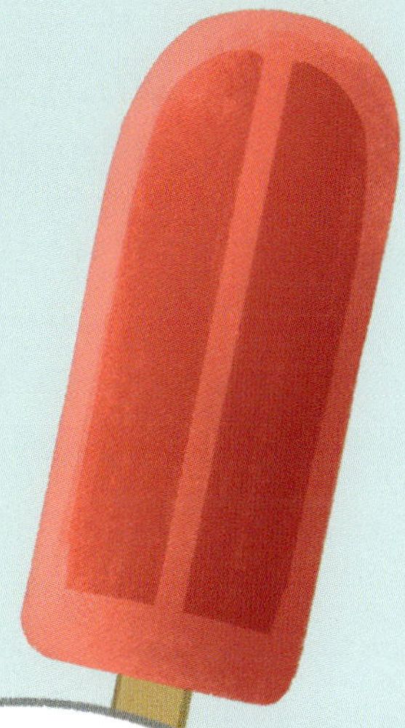

Suck on a soothing ice pop if your throat is really painful.

Eat soft foods that won't hurt your throat.

INFECTIOUS?

Tonsillitis is often linked to colds. When you have a cold, you are infectious. This means that you can easily spread the cold virus to other people when you cough and sneeze. Stay at home until you feel better, cough and sneeze into a tissue, and wash your hands often.

When Maya and her dad get back from the doctor, Maya heads off to bed. Fighting off germs uses up lots of energy, and your body needs plenty of rest.

Maya's throat is too painful for her to eat normal food. Mom and Dad bring her soft foods like soup, mashed potatoes, and yogurt.

The next morning, Maya feels much better. But she's still very tired and her throat still hurts.

After a few days at home, Maya is feeling much better. She can't wait to get back to school and see her friends.

But it's much more exciting than that. When all the students are in their seats, Miss Lindsay takes attendance. Then she makes an announcement.

QUIZ

Now that you've reached the end of this book, how much do you know about getting tonsillitis? Try this quick quiz to find out.

1. Where are your tonsils?
a) In your tummy
b) In your throat
c) In your ear

2. What do your tonsils do?
a) Help fight off germs
b) Help digest your food
c) Help keep you cool

3. What causes tonsillitis?
a) Upset tummy
b) Infected tonsils
c) Shouting

4. Which of these isn't a sign of tonsillitis?
a) Itchy head
b) Sore throat
c) Feeling tired

5. How can you feel better?
a) Get plenty of rest
b) Drink lots of water
c) Suck on an ice pop

Answers:
1. b); 2. a); 3. b); 4. a); 5. All of them

USEFUL WORDS

acetaminophen
Medicine used to treat aches and pains.

antibiotics
Medicines used to treat infections by bacteria.

bacteria
Types of germs that can get inside your body and make you ill.

germs
Very small living things that can cause illnesses.

glands
Parts of the body that can help to fight off germs.

infected
Containing bacteria, viruses, and other germs.

pus
Thick white or yellow liquid produced by the body.

tonsils
Parts of your body that help to fight germs in your throat.

viruses
Types of germs that can get inside your body and make you ill.

USEFUL WEBSITES

https://kidshealth.org/en/kids/tonsillitis.html
Lots of information for you about tonsils and tonsillitis.

https://kidshealth.org/en/parents/tonsillitis.html
Lots of information for your parents about what to do if you have tonsillitis.

ADVICE FOR PARENTS AND CAREGIVERS

Tonsillitis is a common illness, especially among children. It's not infectious, but the infections that often cause it, such as colds, are. Any treatment may depend on whether the tonsillitis is caused by a virus or bacteria. Most cases are caused by viruses and your child should feel better in a few days. If it's caused by a bacterial infection, such as strep throat, a doctor may give your child antibiotics. The doctor should be able to tell the difference by looking at the tonsils and maybe taking a swab test.

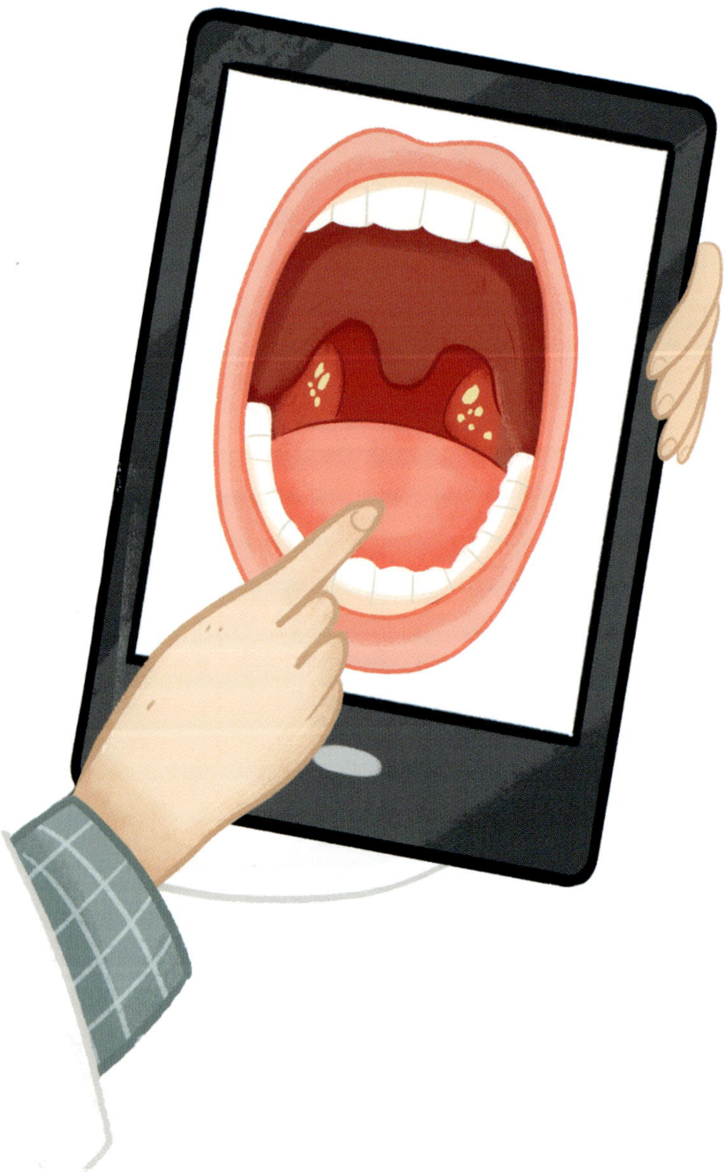

COMPLICATIONS

It is rare to get complications with tonsillitis. Very occasionally, a pocket of pus can form between the tonsil and the throat – this is called a quinsy. Seek urgent medical attention if your child has tonsillitis and is experiencing any of these symptoms:

- A severe sore throat that suddenly gets worse
- Swelling in the mouth or throat
- Difficulty breathing, speaking, or swallowing
- Trouble opening their mouth.

TONSILLECTOMY

An operation to remove the tonsils is called a tonsillectomy. In the past, people often had their tonsils out as children, but today this is much rarer.

A tonsillectomy is usually only recommended if a child has frequent bouts of severe tonsillitis, or the tonsils are so big that they make it hard to breathe at night.

INDEX